PHOTOGRAPHS
THROUGHOUT AMERICAN HISTORY

BY MONIKA DAVIES

Gareth Stevens
PUBLISHING

Please visit our website, www.garethstevens.com. For a free color catalog of all our high-quality books, call toll free 1-800-542-2595 or fax 1-877-542-2596.

Library of Congress Cataloging-in-Publication Data

Names: Davies, Monika, author.
Title: Photographs through American history / Monika Davies.
Description: New York : Gareth Stevens Publishing, [2020] | Series: Journey to the past : investigating primary sources | Includes index.
Identifiers: LCCN 2019006127| ISBN 9781538240502 (pbk.) | ISBN 9781538240526 (library bound) | ISBN 9781538240519 (6 pack)
Subjects: LCSH: United States--History--Pictorial works. | Portrait photography--United States. | Photography in historiography.
Classification: LCC E178.5 .D38 2020 | DDC 973.0022/2--dc23
LC record available at https://lccn.loc.gov/2019006127

First Edition

Published in 2020 by
Gareth Stevens Publishing
111 East 14th Street, Suite 349
New York, NY 10003

Copyright © 2020 Gareth Stevens Publishing

Designer: Katelyn E. Reynolds
Editor: Jill Keppeler

Photo credits: Cover, pp. 1, 7, 9, 11, 12, 13 courtesy of the Library of Congress; cover, pp. 1-32 (wood background) Miro Novak/Shutterstock.com; cover, pp. 1-32 (old paper) Andrey_Kuzmin/Shutterstock.com; pp. 5, 21, 23 (main) Bettmann/Getty Images; p. 15 Alfred Eisenstaedt/The LIFE Picture Collection/Getty Images; p. 16 US archives (https://www.archives.gov/research/ww2/photos/images/ww2-197.jpg)/Yann/ Wikipedia.org; p. 17 Weegee(Arthur Fellig)/International Center of Photography/ Getty Images; p. 19 Universal History Archive/Getty Images; p. 20 Gino Santa Maria/ Shutterstock.com; p. 23 (inset) Michael Zagaris/San Francisco 49ers/Getty Images; p. 24 Julian Kevin Zakaras/Fairfax Media via Getty Images; p. 25 AP Photo/Eddie Adams; p. 26 Bammesk/Wikipedia.org; p. 27 STAN HONDA/AFP/Getty Images; p. 29 Kevin Mazur/WireImage/Getty Images.

Printed in the United States of America

CPSIA compliance information: Batch #CS19GS: For further information contact Gareth Stevens, New York, New York at 1-800-542-2595.

CONTENTS

WORDS IN THE GLOSSARY APPEAR IN **BOLD** TYPE
THE FIRST TIME THEY ARE USED IN THE TEXT.

TRACKING HISTORY

"A photograph is worth a thousand words" is a common phrase. A photograph of a moment in time sometimes can tell a fuller story than many words on a page. Photographs capture the emotions, humanity, and history of a specific moment.

Since the camera's invention, photographs have captured pivotal moments that **defined** and shaped American history. These photographs help us remember and understand American history. Examining photographs can help us understand what the world was like for people in that time period. We might see what difficulties people faced then. Or we may catch a glimpse of the background of a particular historical moment. Let's backtrack into history and see what catches our eye in these photographs!

ANALYZE IT!

WHAT'S HAPPENING IN THIS PHOTOGRAPH? WHY DO YOU THINK IT'S SO FAMOUS?

LUNCH ATOP A SKYSCRAPER

YOU'VE PROBABLY SEEN THIS FAMOUS PHOTOGRAPH BEFORE. THIS 1932 PHOTOGRAPH OF A GROUP OF MEN ENJOYING LUNCH 850 FEET (259 M) ABOVE THE GROUND CAPTURES A FUN—AND TERRIFYING, AT LEAST TO THOSE USED TO KEEPING THEIR FEET ON THE GROUND—MOMENT. THE WORKERS WERE COMPLETING CONSTRUCTION OF A BUILDING AT ROCKEFELLER CENTER IN NEW YORK CITY, BUT THEY TOOK A BREAK TO ENJOY THEIR SANDWICHES (AND POSE FOR A PHOTOGRAPHER)!

WE ONLY KNOW THE IDENTITIES OF TWO MEN IN THIS PHOTOGRAPH. THE WORKER THIRD FROM THE LEFT IS JOE ECKNER, WHILE THE WORKER THIRD FROM THE RIGHT IS JOE CURTIS.

THE 'VANISHING' RACE

This dark, blurry photograph was taken in 1904. The photographer, Edward S. Curtis, was hoping to capture pictures of what he called a "vanishing race"—Native Americans.

This photograph shows a line of Navajo people riding away, their backs to the photographer. Curtis used his photographs and observations to create *The North American Indian*, a set of books about 80 Native American tribes.

While the photographs **documented** a **devastating** time in history for Native Americans, Curtis's books also backed up false and unfair beliefs. Some have said the images are more **stereotypes** of Native American **culture** than **accurate** cultural images. Curtis's pictures showed Native Americans as a "vanishing" race, instead of as a people that survived and are still a part of American society today.

ANALYZE IT!

WHY SHOULD WE CONSIDER THE **BIAS** OF THE PHOTOGRAPHER WHEN LOOKING AT A PHOTOGRAPH?

WESTWARD EXPANSION

AS WHITE SETTLERS BEGAN MOVING WESTWARD ACROSS NORTH AMERICA, IT CAME AT A HEFTY COST TO NATIVE AMERICANS. THESE SETTLERS SOUGHT THE LAND WHERE NATIVE AMERICANS LIVED AND HUNTED. SOON, THE US GOVERNMENT FORCED NATIVE AMERICAN PEOPLES WHO HAD LIVED ON THEIR LANDS FOR CENTURIES TO LEAVE. US TROOPS ATTACKED THOSE WHO RESISTED OR FOUGHT BACK. MANY NATIVE AMERICANS DIED AND MANY WERE FORCED TO MOVE.

EDWARD S. CURTIS SAID THIS PHOTOGRAPH, IN HIS MIND, DEPICTED THE NAVAJO PEOPLE "PASSING INTO THE DARKNESS OF AN UNKNOWN FUTURE."

COTTON MILL GIRL

Historical photographs can show us a piece of the past. However, some photographs also have the power to change history.

In November 1908, Lewis Hine took this photograph of a young girl working in a cotton mill. Hine was an investigative photographer. The National Child Labor Committee hired him to take photographs of young children in poor working conditions in factories. In the early 1900s, it was common to see children working in factories. Almost a fifth of workers in America were 16 or under. These child laborers had long workdays and were paid very little to complete dangerous tasks.

Hine took photographs of children working in factories. He kept track of the children's names and heights on a pad of paper hidden in his pocket.

ANALYZE IT!

WHAT CAN YOU TELL ABOUT THE WORKING CONDITIONS FOR CHILD LABORERS FROM THIS PHOTOGRAPH?

CHANGING MINDS

HINE'S PHOTOGRAPHS EXPOSED THE TERRIBLE WORKING
CONDITIONS CHILD LABORERS FACED. THEY GAVE THE PUBLIC
A GLIMPSE INTO THE FACTORIES, AND THE IMAGES SHOCKED MANY
PEOPLE. HIS PHOTOGRAPHS EVENTUALLY HELPED THE PASSAGE OF CHILD
LABOR LAWS. THE FAIR LABOR STANDARDS ACT WENT INTO EFFECT IN 1938.
IN PART, THIS ACT REGULATES THE YOUNGEST AGES AT WHICH PEOPLE CAN
WORK AND THE CONDITIONS THEY WORK IN.

THIS PHOTOGRAPH SHOWS SADIE PFEIFER. HERE, SHE IS
ONLY 4 FEET (1.2 M) TALL AND APPEARS TINY COMPARED
TO THE DANGEROUS MACHINERY SHE'S WORKING BESIDE.

MIGRANT MOTHER

Dorothea Lange took this iconic photograph, called "Migrant Mother," during the Great Depression in 1936. Lange later wrote of the photograph: "I saw and approached the hungry and desperate mother, as if drawn by a magnet. . . . I did not ask her name or her history. She told me her age, that she was thirty-two.

"She said that they had been living on frozen vegetables from the surrounding fields, and birds that the children killed. She had just sold the tires from her car to buy food. There she sat in that lean-to tent with her children huddled around her, and seemed to know that my pictures might help her, and so she helped me. There was a sort of equality about it."

ANALYZE IT!

WHAT ELSE WAS HAPPENING IN AMERICAN HISTORY AT THE TIME LANGE TOOK THIS PHOTOGRAPH?

THE GREAT DEPRESSION

THE GREAT DEPRESSION WAS A PERIOD OF ECONOMIC TROUBLES IN THE UNITED STATES AND WORLDWIDE FROM 1929 TO 1939. MANY PEOPLE WERE UNEMPLOYED AND MANY WERE POOR, WITHOUT ENOUGH TO EAT OR PROPER SHELTER. IN 1933, THE HEIGHT OF THE GREAT DEPRESSION IN AMERICA, ABOUT 15 MILLION PEOPLE IN THE COUNTRY DIDN'T HAVE A JOB.

DOROTHEA LANGE TOOK THIS PHOTOGRAPH IN NIPOMO, CALIFORNIA, PROBABLY AROUND FEBRUARY OR MARCH 1936.

ANALYZE IT!

HOW DO PHOTOGRAPHS HELP PUT A HUMAN FACE ON HISTORY? HOW DO THESE PHOTOS MAKE YOU FEEL?

The Resettlement Administration (RA), a federal agency, had hired Dorothea Lange to take photographs of poor farmers who were struggling to get enough food for their families. Lange took many photographs during the Great Depression, but the most well-known photograph is that of the "Migrant Mother." The photograph shows the real human consequences of the Great Depression. It shows a mother and her family living in poverty, the despair and uncertainty clear in the mother's face. Soon after, this photograph appeared in newspapers across the country. The photograph became a classic symbol of the poverty experienced by many Americans.

Look closely at the photograph. Do you think Lange purposely narrowed her shot on the face of the mother? How does this affect the emotion shown in this photograph?

DOROTHEA LANGE

FLORENCE OWENS THOMPSON

LANGE TOOK SIX PHOTOGRAPHS TOTAL OF THE FAMILY. THE WOMAN IN THE PHOTOGRAPHS IS FLORENCE OWENS THOMPSON, ALONG WITH A FEW OF HER CHILDREN. THOMPSON HAD SEVEN CHILDREN, ALL OF WHOM SHE WAS STRUGGLING TO FEED. LATER, THOMPSON SAID, "WE JUST EXISTED. ANYWAY, WE LIVED. WE SURVIVED; LET'S PUT IT THAT WAY." SHE AND HER FAMILY DID SURVIVE, BUT SHE NEVER GOT A PENNY FROM ONE OF THE MOST FAMOUS PHOTOGRAPHS EVER TAKEN. SHE DIED IN 1983.

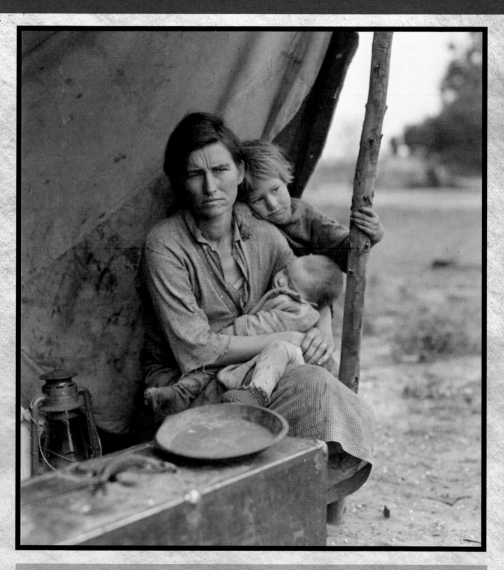

FLORENCE OWENS THOMPSON WAS LIVING AT A CAMPSITE IN THESE PHOTOGRAPHS. SHE WAS TRYING TO FIND WORK AS A PEA PICKER.

V-J KISS IN TIMES SQUARE

This iconic snapshot was taken on August 14, 1945, which marked the end of World War II. World War II was one of the most bloody and costly wars in history, with an estimated 40 million to 50 million deaths worldwide. The war was fought between the Axis powers and the Allies. The Axis powers included Germany, Italy, and Japan, while the Allies were made up of the United States, France, Great Britain, the Soviet Union, and China.

World War II began in 1939 and lasted until 1945. On August 14, the war ended when Japan surrendered. This became known as Victory over Japan, or V-J, Day.

The Allies had won. People all over the United States celebrated. The day was filled with relief and triumph.

ANALYZE IT!

WHY DO YOU THINK THIS PHOTOGRAPH WAS SUCH A POWERFUL IMAGE TO SO MANY?

MIXED FEELINGS

IT WASN'T UNTIL MANY YEARS LATER THAT THE WOMAN IN THE PHOTO WAS IDENTIFIED AS GRETA ZIMMER FRIEDMAN. WHEN ASKED ABOUT THE KISS, SHE SAID, "IT WASN'T A ROMANTIC EVENT. IT WAS JUST AN EVENT OF 'THANK GOD THE WAR IS OVER.'" THE SAILOR JUST GRABBED HER WITHOUT ASKING—AND FOR THAT REASON, SOME PEOPLE HAVE MIXED FEELINGS ABOUT THIS PHOTO TODAY. SOME SEE THE KISS AS AN ASSAULT.

FOR MANY YEARS, PEOPLE BELIEVED THE WOMAN IN THE PHOTOGRAPH WAS A NURSE. HOWEVER, GRETA ZIMMER FRIEDMAN WAS ACTUALLY A DENTAL ASSISTANT AT THE TIME.

ANALYZE IT!

SOMETIMES PHOTOGRAPHERS AND **JOURNALISTS** BECOME PART OF HISTORY EVEN AS THEY OBSERVE. DO YOU THINK THIS IS A GOOD THING?

On V–J Day, celebrations took place across the country. American photographer Alfred Eisenstaedt took this photograph of the spur-of-the-moment kiss. It's one of the most famous images to come from the day, but it's not the only one. Photographer William C. Shrout also took many pictures that day, including photos of Eisenstaedt himself, showing people's joy at the news and how they celebrated.

The picture was taken in Times Square, a major intersection in New York City. Times Square is always a crowded place. However, it's easy to imagine how much more crowded it would have been on V–J Day as Americans celebrated the end of the war. Eisenstaedt's photograph also shows how packed the square was that day.

NAVY PHOTOGRAPHER VICTOR JORGENSEN TOOK THIS PHOTO, WHICH IS VERY SIMILAR TO EISENSTAEDT'S FAMOUS PHOTO.

ALFRED EISENSTAEDT

EISENSTAEDT, WHO WAS BORN IN POLAND, WAS A SELF-TAUGHT PHOTOGRAPHER WHO HAD A LONG, SUCCESSFUL CAREER IN THE UNITED STATES AND OTHER COUNTRIES. ON AUGUST 14, 1945, HE WAS ALSO CELEBRATING THE END OF THE WAR ALONGSIDE OTHER AMERICANS. WHILE HE WAS DOCUMENTING THE DAY USING HIS CAMERA, HE WOUND UP BEING PART OF HISTORY, TOO. HIS FELLOW PHOTOGRAPHER SHROUT TOOK PHOTOS OF HIM KISSING A WOMAN IN CELEBRATION.

PHYSICISTS HAVE TRIED TO FIGURE OUT WHAT TIME THE PHOTOGRAPH WAS TAKEN, AS ALFRED EISENSTAEDT COULDN'T REMEMBER. THEY'VE CONCLUDED THE PHOTOGRAPH WAS TAKEN AT EXACTLY 5:51 P.M.

ROSA PARKS'S
ARREST

Rosa Parks's name awakens thoughts of the civil rights movement during the 1950s and 1960s. During this time, many people began demanding equal rights for African Americans and others.

Also during this time, Jim Crow laws still were enforced in many southern US states. These were laws that enforced segregation, or the forced separation of races. Some of these laws included segregation on public transportation. For example, in Alabama, white citizens sat at the front of the bus, while black citizens had to sit in certain seats at the back of the bus.

On December 1, 1955, in Montgomery, Alabama, Parks stepped onto a bus after she'd finished work for the day. She sat in one of the designated seats at the back of the bus.

ANALYZE IT!

WHAT DO YOU THINK
ROSA PARKS IS FEELING
IN THIS PHOTOGRAPH?

OTHER JIM CROW LAWS

JIM CROW LAWS HAD HUGE EFFECTS ON DAY-TO-DAY LIFE FOR AFRICAN AMERICANS. SOME LAWS ENFORCED SEGREGATION IN RESTAURANTS, AT WATER FOUNTAINS, IN RESTROOMS, AND EVEN IN CEMETERIES. THESE LAWS OFTEN RESTRICTED AFRICAN AMERICANS FROM LIVING IN "WHITE" NEIGHBORHOODS. MARRIAGE WASN'T ALLOWED BETWEEN WHITE AND BLACK CITIZENS. THE LAWS REFLECTED AND ENCOURAGED A **RACIST** AGENDA IN MANY STATES.

ROSA PARKS LATER SAID, "I DID NOT GET ON THE BUS TO GET ARRESTED; I GOT ON THE BUS TO GO HOME." SHE WAS FINED $10 AND HAD TO PAY AN ADDITIONAL $4 IN COURT FEES.

ANALYZE IT!

WHAT DO YOU THINK
ROSA PARKS IS THINKING
IN THE PHOTOGRAPH TO
THE RIGHT, TAKEN MORE
THAN A YEAR AFTER
THE LAST ONE?

A white man then got on the bus, but he wasn't able to find a seat at the front. The driver told Parks and three other black citizens to give up their seats for the white passenger—and Parks refused.

This refusal led to Parks's arrest. The photograph on the previous page is her booking photo, a stark black-and-white image that shows her **defiantly** looking at the camera with her booking number. This photograph captures a piece of this historic moment in time. Parks was only one of many citizens who fought for equal rights, but she started a movement with her bravery that day.

Parks's arrest directly led to the Montgomery bus boycott. She later became known as the "mother of the civil rights movement."

YOU CAN SEE A
MONTGOMERY CITY BUS
JUST LIKE THE ONE
ROSA PARKS RODE IN
AT THE NATIONAL
CIVIL RIGHTS MUSEUM
IN MEMPHIS, TENNESSEE.

MONTGOMERY BUS BOYCOTT

THE MONTGOMERY BUS BOYCOTT TOOK PLACE FROM DECEMBER 5, 1955, TO DECEMBER 20, 1956. A BOYCOTT IS THE ACT OF REFUSING TO HAVE DEALINGS WITH A PERSON OR BUSINESS IN ORDER TO TRY TO FORCE CHANGE. DURING THIS PERIOD, AFRICAN AMERICANS REFUSED TO USE BUS TRANSPORTATION. ON DECEMBER 20, 1956, THE US SUPREME COURT UPHELD THE DECISION OF A LOWER COURT THAT HAD RULED THAT BUSES AND OTHER TRANSPORTATION COULDN'T BE SEGREGATED.

THIS PHOTOGRAPH WAS TAKEN OVER A YEAR AFTER ROSA PARKS'S ARREST. SHE SITS AT THE FRONT OF THE BUS ON DECEMBER 21, 1956, FOLLOWING THE SUPREME COURT DECISION TO END SEGREGATION ON BUSES.

BLACK POWER
SALUTE

The date was October 16, 1968. Tommie Smith and John Carlos, two American athletes, had just won the gold and bronze medals in the 200-meter dash at the Summer Olympics in Mexico City

As "The Star-Spangled Banner" began playing, the two men bowed their heads and raised their fists, on which they wore black gloves. Photographer John Dominis quickly took a photo. The moment was seen as an acknowledgement of the black power movement. The salute had a clear statement. To the world, it was saying that before the men could salute the United States, the country had to treat black citizens the same as white citizens.

If you examine the photograph closely, you might notice several symbols that show their fight for equality. Which ones stand out to you?

ANALYZE IT!

PEOPLE ARE STILL PROTESTING A LACK OF EQUAL RIGHTS TODAY. HOW ARE THESE IMAGES SIMILAR?

PETER NORMAN

AUSTRALIAN PETER NORMAN WAS THE SILVER MEDALIST IN THE PHOTOGRAPH. ALTHOUGH HE DIDN'T RAISE HIS FIST, HE STOOD IN SOLIDARITY WITH SMITH AND CARLOS. HE ALSO WORE AN OLYMPIC PROJECT FOR HUMAN RIGHTS BADGE IN SUPPORT. LATER, HE WAS ASKED TO CONDEMN THEIR ACTIONS. HE REFUSED, AND HE WAS **OSTRACIZED** IN HIS COMMUNITY. NORMAN DIED IN 2006. SMITH AND CARLOS CARRIED HIS COFFIN AT HIS FUNERAL.

RAISED HAND WITH GLOVE
UNITY OF BLACK AMERICA AND BLACK POWER

SCARF
BLACK PRIDE

OPEN JACKET
SOLIDARITY WITH BLUE-COLLAR WORKERS

BADGE
OLYMPIC PROJECT FOR HUMAN RIGHTS

COLIN KAEPERNICK AND OTHER NFL PLAYERS KNEELING IN 2016

SMITH LATER SAID, "I WAS PROUD OF THE COUNTRY, BUT EVEN THE GREATEST THINGS IN THE WORLD NEED ATTENTION WHEN THEY'RE NOT AS STRONG AS THEY COULD BE. IT WAS A CRY FOR FREEDOM."

BOAT OF NO SMILES

Eddie Adams was a photographer known for caring about his subjects' dignity, or sense of pride and self-respect. One of his most famous photographs is titled "Boat of No Smiles." In the 1977 photo, a Vietnamese **refugee** holds her sleeping son. A sense of hopelessness is clear.

"Boat of No Smiles" was taken near Thailand. The subjects are all South Vietnamese refugees trying to escape Communist Vietnam, seeking a safe place to live. There were 50 refugees, all crowded into a fishing boat. They'd been floating in the sea for days at that point. They weren't allowed into Thailand, as some countries refuse to take in refugees. Adams took their photo to show the world what they were going through.

ANALYZE IT!

IN WHAT WAYS DO YOU THINK A PHOTOGRAPH HAS THE POWER TO CHANGE HISTORY?

EDDIE ADAMS

PHOTOS FOR CHANGE

EDDIE ADAMS'S PHOTOGRAPHS WERE PUBLISHED IN MANY PLACES. IN PART BECAUSE OF THEM, US PRESIDENT JIMMY CARTER SENT THE US NAVY TO HELP THE REFUGEES, AND THE US CONGRESS OFFERED A SAFE HOME FOR THEM—INCLUDING THE PEOPLE IN THIS PHOTOGRAPH—IN THE UNITED STATES. FROM 1978 TO 1981, THE UNITED STATES ADMITTED MORE THAN 200,000 REFUGEES FROM VIETNAM.

EDDIE ADAMS TITLED THIS PHOTOGRAPH "BOAT OF NO SMILES" BECAUSE IT WAS THE FIRST TIME HE TOOK A PHOTOGRAPH AND NO ONE SMILED.

RAISING THE FLAG AT
GROUND ZERO

September 11, 2001, is remembered as a dark day in American history. **Terrorists** took over four US commercial airplanes, crashing two of the planes into the World Trade Center in New York City and one into the Pentagon in Washington, DC. The fourth plane crashed into a field in Pennsylvania. Nearly 3,000 people died in the attacks and afterward.

The photograph displayed at right shows three firefighters raising an American flag at the World Trade Center site as smoke rises from the wreckage.

The image reminded many people of another famous photograph, one taken in 1945 on the Japanese island of Iwo Jima. That photo showed five US Marines and a sailor raising the American flag. Newspaper photographer Joe Rosenthal took that photo.

ANALYZE IT!

WHY DO YOU THINK BOTH THESE IMAGES BECAME SO FAMOUS AND SO POPULAR?

RAISING THE FLAG ON IWO JIMA
BY JOE ROSENTHAL

THE PHOTOGRAPHER'S
POINT OF VIEW

NEWSPAPER PHOTOGRAPHER THOMAS E. FRANKLIN TOOK THE
9/11 PHOTOGRAPH. HE LATER SAID, "THIS PICTURE DID NOT
STAND OUT TO ME. THREE MEN RAISING A FLAG PALED IN COMPARISON
TO THOUSANDS OF PEOPLE DYING AND TWO BUILDINGS FALLING TO THE
GROUND. I CAN'T EVEN SAY THIS IS THE BEST PICTURE I EVER TOOK. IT IS
THE PHOTO WITH THE MOST MEANING."

THE GROUND ZERO PHOTOGRAPH FEATURES THREE NEW YORK FIREFIGHTERS:
GEORGE JOHNSON, DAN MCWILLIAMS, AND BILLY EISENGREIN.

A MOMENT IN TIME

Studying photographs is one way for us to examine and understand history. However, it's also important to remember a photograph shows us only a moment in time. We can't see the before and after of most photographs. However, photographs still have power to take us back to that point in time in some ways. Using photographs as primary sources is a great way to step back into history.

Think about the photographs in this book. Which ones moved you the most? Did any make you reconsider your beliefs about a certain moment in time?

A powerful photograph can humanize history or document an important moment. Today, we live in a time of selfies and smartphones. Everyday people, like you, now increasingly join professional photographers in capturing history.

ANALYZE IT!

HOW DO YOU THINK THE CHANGING WAYS OF PHOTOGRAPHY WILL CHANGE THE PRIMARY SOURCES OF THE FUTURE?

THE CHANGING WORLD
OF PHOTOGRAPHY

THE WORLD OF PHOTOGRAPHY HAS DEVELOPED A GREAT
DEAL OVER THE YEARS. ONCE, ALL CAMERAS USED FILM TO TAKE
PICTURES. PHOTOGRAPHERS HAD TO CAREFULLY THINK ABOUT THEIR
PHOTOGRAPHS, SINCE THEY ONLY HAD SO MUCH FILM AVAILABLE AT ANY
GIVEN TIME. NOW, MOST PEOPLE OWN SMARTPHONES THAT CAN TAKE THOUSANDS
OF PHOTOS WITH A CLICK OF THE BUTTON! STILL, PHOTOGRAPHY SKILLS ARE
IMPORTANT. THEY CAN HELP SOMEONE COMPOSE A PHOTOGRAPH TO CAPTURE
EMOTIONS AND MOMENTS IN HISTORY.

TV PERSONALITY ELLEN DEGENERES, RIGHT, POSES FOR SELFIES WITH FANS
IN THIS 2015 PHOTO TAKEN AT THE PEOPLE'S CHOICE AWARDS.
SELFIES CAN BE PRIMARY SOURCES, TOO!

GLOSSARY

accurate: the state of being free from mistakes

bias: a belief that some people or ideas are better than others

culture: the beliefs and ways of life of a group of people

defiant: showing a tendency to challenge, resist, or fight

define: to show or describe something clearly

devastating: causing widespread damage

document: to record in writing or other media

journalist: someone who works with the collecting, writing, and editing of news stories for newspapers, magazines, websites, television, or radio

ostracize: to not allow someone to be included

racist: someone who believes that one race is better than another or others

refugee: someone who is seeking a safe place to live, especially during a time of war

stereotype: an often unfair and untrue belief that many people have about all people or things of a certain kind

terrorist: one who uses violence and fear to challenge an authority

FOR MORE
INFORMATION

BOOKS

Honovich, Nancy. *Guide to Photography.* Washington, DC: National Geographic Society, 2015.

Life Editors. *A Story of America in 100 Photographs.* New York, NY: Life, 2018.

Meyerowitz, Joel. *Seeing Things: A Kid's Guide to Looking at Photographs.* New York, NY: Aperture Foundation, 2016.

WEBSITES

Analyze a Photograph
www.archives.gov/education/lessons/worksheets/photo.html
Learn how to make sense of a photograph and its features.

40 Intriguing Photos to Make Students Think
www.nytimes.com/2016/09/22/learning/40-intriguing-photos-to-make-students-think.html
Test yourself and try to figure out what's going on in these 40 photographs.

The Most Influential Images of All Time
100photos.time.com
Look at TIME Magazine's 100 images that "changed the world."

INDEX